T0161528

Pasolini's Our

Pasolini's Our

Nathanaël

Nightboat Books
New York

© 2018 by Nathanaël
All rights reserved
Printed in the United States

ISBN: 978-1-937658-90-8

Design and cover collage by Kit Schluter
Cover features modified portrait of Pier Paolo Pasolini by Anatole Saderman
Text set in Minion Pro

Cataloging-in-publication data is available
From the Library of Congress

Nightboat Books
New York
www.nightboat.org

—una fragilità

It's like it rains in the city and the sewers are backed up. The water rises, but the water is innocent, it's rainwater, it has neither the fury of the sea nor the wickedness of a river current. [...] But it rises and it drowns you.

PIER PAOLO PASOLINI

The interment of the bird is a flight of the imagination, which would soar, if it could, on wings without beating.

PASOLINI'S OUR

*But why then such an image from
his face and from his body?*

JEAN GENET

¶ In none of Pasolini's films does it rain. I can affirm that it rains in Visconti, there is the rain and the absence of the rain; in Sokurov it rains on the face of Shostakovich; it rains as well in Jean-Pierre Melville, on the sea and the public square; in Carol Reed it rains, it rains wondrously inside and out; in Michael Curtiz it rains abundantly on the faces of the lovers, the aeroplane and the strip; it rains in Jia Zhangke, on the blood and the street; in Orson Welles it rains on the mud, México; Jules Dassin, by night, it rains, and on Richard Widmark, the city; in Shindo Kaneto, Michelangelo Antonioni, Marguerite Duras; in Duras it rains and in Jean-Luc Godard, Boris Ingster and Fritz Lang, it rains, it rains, a name and it rains, John Boorman, Rithy Panh, Kurosawa Akira, G. W. Pabst, Sergio Sollima. It rains in David Lean, at the train station. John Ford and Agnès Varda. Elia Kazan.

The cinema seems only to wait for the rain, it waits only for that, for it to rain, on the screen and the skin, for the cinema itself to rain, even in times of drought, the cinema rains.

In none of Pasolini's films does it rain. I say so without assurance and with the unshakable assurance of this particular certainty: no rain in Pasolini.

What I am saying is a discrepancy.

The discrepancy, to begin with, of the voice.

I am in agreement with myself as to this discrepancy, and make it heard.

No rain in Pasolini.

¶ Perhaps, no exile, either.

¶ I said that I would find the fault in the imagination, when it was the fault that had supplanted me. I had imagined it that way. I went toward that which I had said to myself, with an entirely untakeable voice, a voice that had its share of ocean, and its share of drownings, of drownings, of capsize, of archipelagos and of dying reefs. Of birds floating at its surface, sticky with petrol, songless, flightless, strangled by the hands of humans who were dying also. It was a manner of fault, a fault until proven otherwise, contrary, and due to all the other faults of history, where the names also drown and capsize, in order to have a taste of exactly what will have drawn them, there, obviously. History, such as it isn't said, lent to no voice, and conditioned by the often imperceptible tremors that displace the assurance of footsteps that climb, each time, the same hill. After, down below, there is the slope of the hill, an unexpected opening, a sun that doesn't reach in, the passerines, and the rail line, overlooked. The leaves, their rustling. No, there is no wind. Nor any presage. Just, and only just, the sense of having missed something urgent.

¶ We laid down on the tracks. We didn't dare speak. Still we said that the track, in itself, was a sort of vivisection, not only of the city, but of pain. We agreed that the meeting should take place in secret. We buried objects of no value in pebbled earth, and we anticipated the inevitable rendering of our effects, spat up here and there. We took care that the war, enclosed in our bodies, should remain driven there, the body, a falling point, the voice, an imagination maintained by the sole skin of thought.

¶ We translated. One and another. And ourselves. It was a first attempt. A first failure. In the form, perhaps, of an embrace. We embraced in that which precisely was refused us. Gently, and with dejection.

¶ It went without saying that none of this was unspeakable. That on the contrary we had said too much. Overly insisted. Overly tormented the language with our infallible defeat.

¶ I say we but it was a decomposed we. The bodies distributed across several continents. Some along a river. Others seeking a desert. Still others, gray already, and lacking chlorophyll, adopted a stone place, of gravel or cement. Regardless. All drew their supply from the tracks, autopsied themselves.

¶ Of water or glass. Of sand and of sadness.

¶ The marsh all trembling with what it was.

Il Doppiaggio

In the Italian cinema1[1] the voice is a grafted voice. The lines are pronounced at least twice. There is the voice of the shoot, in every imaginable language. Then there is the voice of doubling. All voices are dubbed. There is the dubbing of the other and the doubling of the self. In *La Riccotta*, Orson Welles speaks his words in Italian. After, another mouth extends as far

---

1.   From about 1939 to 1968.

as his, attributing to him that funny little voice.[2] A decision Pasolini regretted: a false-dubbing, or else a dubbing too centred on the authenticity—of the regional accent—at the cost of the singularity of Welles's voice, resorbed into the void of the erased celluloid. Fidelity to what? All voices are voice-overs, even and especially those—Monica Vitti, Clint Eastwood, Lee Van Cleef, Franco Citti, Eli Wallach, Marcelo Mastroianni...— which sometimes dub themselves. Italian film has (at least) two time signatures, the time of the image, and the time of the voice. Here, there is, necessarily, a discrepancy. Even in total agreement.

¶ *Il doppiaggio*: a sort of di-vestment, of the face, where the mouth lends itself to a deformity that is specific, not only to language, but to speech, a speech that is returned to the mouth without ever leaving it, raising in this way an impassable limit that the body is repeatedly called upon to imitate, in order to arrive at an impression of its remission. Originating from nothing, and from nowhere, like Werner Herzog's hill, that invites *no one to nothing*; *hier*, says his German sentence, *here*, »Dieser Hügel hier lädt niemanden zu nichts«, and the French versant of which retains *nothing*, disposing of the discomfiture of *niemanden*. *Of the person* of *no one*. « Cette colline n'invite à rien. »[3]

¶ A sea sickness, say. Without the necessary words to say it.

---

2.   It is the voice of Giorgio Bassani.
3.   Werner Herzog, *Vom Gehen im Eis*, München, Hanser, 2012 [1978], p. 12. In French, *Sur le chemin des glaces*, tr. Anne Dutter, 1979, p. 17. In English, *Of Walking in Ice*, tr. Martje Herzog and Alan Greeberg, 1980.

¶ Without *anteriority*, and at all times accounted for.

¶ The cinema is a glass pane. This is how it disabuses the mirror. Vertical or aslant, it takes the light, it takes the shadow, it burns grass and stone, it burns the river in its unmade bed. It is a manner of knowledge, a manner of deceiving the eyes, of pacifying the heights and throwing them down. The heat waves, the air currents, winds of sea and land, and the small deaths assembled by the wreck at the foot of its technicity.

¶ Idiotically, and at all ages, one runs into it, a wall without visible contours, and without materiality, that the eye traverses without incident, drawing the body with it, the body that is taken—for we are taken in—and which has already crossed through, glass and skull, there must be blood, the bruise, and the cry or stumble, to be able at last to seize hold of the sense of the limit which has run into us. *A posteriori* and without accusation.

¶ Without anteriority, in other words without resentment.

¶ It rains the cinema. A glassy rain resurfaced from the regions of a gaze, arrested, precisely, in the voice. I tender my hand to listen. I shut myself up in the cubicle and I remove my clothes. I remove the voice first, then the rest. I imagine myself this way. Fragile breakaway of fluids. Starfish or anemone, I flourish, in the muck and the salt waters. Curls of foam and scattering of mosquitoes. The extent of the ponds as far as the eye can see, in other words where sight becomes lost in misleading contradictions, against the view of an imagined thing. It's

true, once, I put my feet in it, sinking in to my knees, and the
sky gave the impression of having neared. When it was the
road that was crushing me.

¶ Herons and sandpipers, salt-marshes with your brackish
waters: never have you been photographed.

In Praise of Nothing

> *The single thing proves over and over again to be
> unimportant, but the possibility of every single
> thing reveals something about the nature of the
> world.*

LUDWIG WITTGENSTEIN

¶ So what: the voice, the rain and the cinema. I had come to
speak of photography. Of the sole effort of transcribing, with
light, and through a chemical process, an image on glass,
metal, paper. I laid the body out on the track. I unbuttoned. I
gave time the task of watering a face, a swath of clothing. As
for the voice, it found itself consigned to a work of scraping.
There are things, which, buried in a too violently laboured
soil, out of modesty or despair, sink to depths that are un-
fathomable to the instruments designed for such a purpose.
Even the naked eye, nonetheless trained to this identificatory,
can only be mistaken. It is not enough to see or to look at nor
even to know how to see, a fossilised corpse.

¶ There is this which you are likely better attuned to than I and which is owed to a single word. An archaism, without a doubt, in this era of overcome ages, which goes back at least as far as the track, as the wall, as the ditch.

¶ No, I have come to praise nothing.

¶ An obsolescence, the way one would say an outbreak—of an illness or a situation or the human body. Latent, like the image, deepened and traversed by words which aren't able, to say so.

¶ One can affirm, I think, with regard to photography, that it is obsolete already. Driven already into its own history. That to excavate it from there where it has burst into so many shards, one requires recourse to more than a gaze. One can say of it that it is dead already, of its own death, and fantasied as a present within reach of the voice, always doubled. That even a translation is incapable of rescuing it from there. And that the desire to fish it out is a defunct desire, which belongs to a form of vitality that is no longer current, in this age of crumbling massifs.

¶ Suspended between two instances of its morbidity.

¶ To take it is to belie it. To give it is to annul it.

¶ It is thus in obsolescence that I address you, with my own voice, and procedures of location to which we are accustomed, which begin with the eye and often end there. Yet, like the nematode—the eye worm, *loa loa*—it often arrives from another region of the body. It arrives from the body and becomes unrecognisable to it.

¶ The wall, like the glass pane, is properly speaking comprised of *two walls*, just as the two surfaces of the glass grant it two distinct walls, between which, when looking closely, one can sometimes discern an air bubble, which belongs neither to one surface nor to the other, but indeed to both at once; unbreathable, this bubble is a capital punishment, both of the air, and of the glass, which is transformed without decision into a gallows, and that is precisely where seeing is defused.

¶ *Grenze*, says German, to designate the boundary, *frontière*, in French, *frontiera* in Italian, and above all else, the ear receives, and transmits, the singularity of this border, of this limit, of this demarcation. The language develops the habit of this singular, and the mouth is thus advised.

¶ Have we not all been saying, for years, and still today, as though re-memoried, *the* Berlin Wall?

¶ And yet the Austrian philosopher would have it otherwise; he says »Die grenzen meiner sprache bedeuten die grenzen meiner welt«.[4]

¶ It was a misapprehension of a banality.

---

4.   *The limits of my language mean the limits of my world.* Ludwig Wittgenstein, *Tractatus Logico-Philosophicus*, tr. C.K. Ogden [and Frank Ramsay and G.E. Moore with the author], London, Routledge, 1922, p. 148.

¶ Because the wall, in all of its murderous materiality, was above all else an idea, the illusion of a very real thing, and like all reality, when confronted with language, in other words its dictatorship, it was out of reach—of the eye and the body. Here—*hier*—whosoever crosses the border is thrown out of the world.

¶ « ... for [citizens of the East] the concrete edifice which the West perceived as 'The Wall' was just the last element in a deeply-ranged sequence of obstacles. Those who actually managed to advance from the East to the West had to negotiate sign-posted restricted areas patrolled by police and state security officers, followed by various perimeter defences and the hinterland Wall, before they found themselves in the death-strip of the border fortifications proper; a death-strip patrolled by the soldiers of the Border Command [...] » (12)[5]

¶ Let us remove the worm from the eye. And return the organ to its blind.

Hinterland I

¶ *Often, we made the mistake of attributing to language a descriptive pre-eminence. Just like the Austrian philosopher, or perhaps following too closely, and likely misunderstanding his language, drawn as it was, between an inconvenient German and an English repeatedly reframed according to an*

5.   Axel Klausmeier and Leo Schmidt, *Wall Remnants—Wall Traces*, tr. Ralf Jaeger, with Claire Benett and Karoline Kristen, Berlin / Bonn, Westkreuz-Verlag, 2004, p. 12.

experience of renewed traversals, and arterial wars, trans-
lating and retranslating, the so-called impassable limits of
experience, we fell at the foot of his untimely letter, destined
to its solitude. That is what we gave ourselves to, in the dis-
persal and tear of dreams, in the swellings of history such as
it is told and recorded, in the fragile inscription of the dust's
scratchings on the cornea. Disabused, in other words atheist to
incurred experiences, and just like the butterfly whose wings
are seized in flight, pressed between two pieces of glass for
the sole purpose of our own auscultation. If the moon incites
dreams of the body, the photograph of the moon breaks an
inoffensive glass. With the simplest of anger's gestures, thrown
against a ground, in order to verify its perfect fragility. There
is no such thing as the threshold on which we are broken.

Hinterland II

¶ What did he do? He photographed it. Through the layer-
ing of four faces, he peeled back their singularities, making
of the single face imprinted on paper, a counterfeit: the
counterfeit of the image itself. By exposing the stratification
of faces as of different geological layers, what emerges, far
from being an *appearance of appurtenance*, is the equivalent
of an incision into the seven layers of skin—a blood draw,
vital, mortal, poisoning, and whose scarred trace speaks at
length of its traversals. It isn't the image that says so, but
the falsification of the image, of the properties attributed
to it. The photograph of a photograph is a skin torn back.

"When it rains in a city"

¶ The French language doesn't settle. When faced with the word *Todesstreifen*, designating the death strip in question, it hesitates between several designations, none of which is able to fix the identity of this liminal zone. Among the references to this element of the Wall, comprised, we now know, of several walls—of walls, of miradors, of patrol paths, of lamp posts, protection barriers, minefields, of fences and dogs, obstacles of all kinds—one encounters at least three referential formulas in French—including the visceral « ruban de la mort »; the more crude « bande de la mort » (with its aggressive and explicitly predatory sexual connotation); and sometimes even the « couloir de la mort », language that is habitually assigned to *death row* of the United States—the only country in the Americas, with the sole exception of Saint-Kitts and Nevis, to still practise the death penalty.

¶ The hanging wall is a counter-part.

¶ Elsewhere, the no-man's land of the death strip hesitates as to the attribution of the mined passage. Impassible, the site extrapolates as to the untranslatability of such an experience, and distinguishes itself historically—and symbolically—from other walls of national sequestration erected in hatred enshrined by the law: whether the Roman *Limes*, the Great Wall of China, the *Geder HaHafrada*—or wall of racial segregation as it is called in Palestine—or again the Border Wall between the United States and Mexico.[6] The face is obliterated.

---

6.   These ramparts, "walls of appropriation before being walls of property" (p. 9).

¶ In the absence of the dead there is recourse to the ceno-taph. That is where the irreducible death of death is buried, which will, incidentally, be covered in names, often invented for the occasion of such levelling. It should have been: *in the absence of a body*. But the very word *cenotaph* anticipates that which it is incumbent upon it to ratify.

¶ The word *Streifen* can cause confusion to the inexperienced eye, for there is at once the taction or grazing of the lowercase *streifen*, alongside the striations of the uppercase *Streifen*, in other words its stripes or rays. Be that as it may, it carries an altogether consequential sense for the divided wall. It is that *Streifen* recalls, deep in its word, its epidermal dimension, in other words: its skin.

¶ *Streifen*, one says, *Filmstreifen*.

¶ Must one see in Stalin's lawn which the border guards re-ferred to as an asparagus bed—"a straw mat bristling with fourteen-centimetre long points,"[7] in other words one of the many constitutive obstacles of the *Berliner Mauer*—the exemplar of this filmic facture, whose adjacent sandy soil served to register the negative footprints of the fugitives?

¶ A drop in blood pressure in the form of birds fallen from flight appals you. At the precise spot at which you were await-

---

are all walls of exclusion, and despite the intensification of their delineation, none has (yet) dislodged of its symbolic value the Berlin Wall whose fall in 1989 con-secrated its importance. Claude Quétel, *Histoire des murs*, Paris, Éditions Perrin, 2012.

7.   *"Emmurés!' — la frontière interallemande.* Berlin, Deutsche Welle + Stiftung Berliner Mauer, 2009, colour (11:00).

ed. And your voice, which drifted after you, like a squall of smoke, revealed the whole of your offence. It was both an offence of truth, and of convoy. I saw it all. I wrote none of it down. Because I wanted, with me, for this truth to die. The truth of birds fallen from the sky. One imagines that no one—*Niemand*—will have thought to bury them.[8]

¶ At the last, photography is caught in the trap of disfigurement. November 9, 1989, when under the pressure of the crowds, the guards of the Berlin Wall were ceding the border in breaches, they rapidly executed an ostentatiously impotent procedure, whereby the most turbulent *Ostberliner* were extracted from the throngs, and in order, subsequently, to identify them, had their passports stamped *over the photograph*, affixing the seal of the border police *on the faces* of the most demonstrative among them. The photographic evidence is without ambiguity. It is a (desperate) act of disfigurement. A disfigurement which served, within several hours of the fall of the Berlin Wall, to block the way back to those who proclaimed themselves to be *passing*.

¶ The *Todesstreifen*, at its untimely hour, is caught *in flagrante delicto* of its semantics.

---

8.   "Niemand gibt uns eine Chance." David Bowie and Brian Eno, "Helden," in *Heroes / Helden*, RCA, 1977 (6:07).

DAYS OF BROKEN LEAD

I ran under the sun, because I saw the image.

INGEBORG BACHMAN

¶ When she comes down the paper tears into pieces of glass.[9]

¶ A body of fragments and of shards, of bones and of shreds. A body said to be *without a sex* and outlaw of its word, released into the void until the rope is taut.

¶ The question of white glass surely falls under the philosopher's competence. Its opacity is owed to tin oxide, calcium antimonate, and arsenic oxide.

¶ Do you know that it rains inside that mortuary sand, that the mouth transmuted into a porcelain surrogate kisses the very fissure of its flash in order to ensure its precipitation into history?

¶ When it falls I keep from naming myself.

¶ Stained glass restoration techniques are numerous throughout Europe and are the subject of detailed studies. As to the necessity for this practice, its scale and scope, the quality of the material employed, its application under heat or under cold, and the method retained for the eventual resuscitation of colour, the cleansing or abandon of the original glass, the eventual application of a layer of concealed plastic. Volume 1 of *Bulletin Monumental* (1959) published in France considers these questions at length, thanks, notably to the research carried out by a chemist, an archaeologist and a physicist, whose findings are surveyed in *Teka konserwatorska*, a Polish journal published in 1956. If France was less liable,

9. "a dead paper, without age" (Ingeborg Bachmann, from the French translation, slightly modified). *Franza*, tr. Miguel Couffon, Arles, Actes Sud, 1985, p. 163.

at that time, to abandon traditional restoration techniques because of the material abundance of this artefact, even if it meant considerable loss, the less widespread stained glass of 14th century Toruń and Chełmno, for example, relocated in the 19th century to a castle in Malborg, are entitled to every manner of consideration. A survey of practices employed by various European countries, including England, Switzerland, Belgium or Austria, reveals considerable divergences.

¶ The relay between these practices, grafted onto a map of Europe where the rail lines, whose murderous charge has scarcely dissipated, registers against its correspondences the full sense of the *our* in question, its rupture and dislocation.

¶ As Rem Koolhaas recalls, by tracing the perilous journey, between the Spanish Civil War and the Third Reich, of elements of Mies van der Rohe's Barcelona Pavilion at the 1929 World's Fair: "The train journey was complicated. The railway tracks of each country were of different widths; many transfers were needed."[10]

¶ If the inclemencies provoked by changes in track gauge[11] furnish a sort of radiography of Europe in the days of *dead glass* as the trade indicates,[12] it is through a historiographic process

10. *Rem Koolhaa*s, « Less is More : Installation for the 1986 Milan Triennale, Italy, 1985 » in Rem Koolhaas and Bruce Mau, *Small, medium, large, extra-large Office for Metropolitan Architecture*, New York, Monacelli Press, 1996, p. 54.
11. ...not to mention the difference between signalling systems employed by one country or another, or else the divergences between norms of electrification.
12. The facades of the German pavilion are made of glass. The building is also comprised of steel, marble, (Roman) travertine and onyx elements. Rem Koolhaas will reconstruct a modified version of the pavilion at the XVIIth Triennale di Milano, 1986.

similar to the optical illusion implemented in the restorative works of medieval stained glass; in other words recourse to the *doubling* of the primary matter by a piece of white glass whose armature will be determined by the current practices of a given context as well as the marked preference of the artisan.

¶ *Il mare era ferma come una lastra.*[13]

¶ The layers of glass attesting to different cultural, not to say geological, periods sample the dusts caught in time, an eternal present unsteadied by the eye. A time the extent of whose abyss is blindingly visible and infinitely traced, if not translated.

¶ It is the rain that devitrifies, by dissolving the alkaline parcels of matter, in order to restore its sandy opacity.

¶ Between *death* and the *hand*, between the ancient glass and *suo doppio*, the eye is charged with the full expression of its disappointment. Say it is situated between two propositions the distance between which is disavowed:

"I saw something."   and   "I have no sex,"[14]

¶ Remove the stone, the glass remains to be photographed.

¶ It is Kawabata Yasunari who, in a text entitled "Kinjū," ("Of Birds and Beasts") avers: "There are birds among the very young of which it is impossible to distinguish male from female. Dealers bring whole nests down from the mountains,

13. Pier Paolo Pasolini. *Racconti Romani.* Paris, Éditions Gallimard, 2002 [1995], p. 113.
14. Ingeborg Bachmann, from the French. *op. cit.*, p. 162.

but as soon as they can recognise them they throw away the females which will not sell because they do not sing."[15]

¶ *Una lastra* speaks all at once the (metal) plate, the stone (slab) or the (opaque, transparent) pane. It also articulates, in common parlance, the radiography, proffering the *still* narrative of successive materials, from the writing machine to the dreamed *insula*.

¶ By night, the building is lit with sodium, the body floats in a lead mesh. The neighbourhood drowns in insomnia, its fists beating the door from its hinge.

¶ I have no reason to be dismayed. We have entered into history.

15. *House of the Sleeping Beauties and other stories*, tr. Edward Seidensticker (modified). Tokyo, Kodansha International, 1969, p. 133.

THE CRY OF THE CHRYSANTHEMUM

When reality is confronted with the void, when the void brushes up against the real, we cannot hold back our surprise, and we cry out [...]: Why?

KUKI SHŪZŌ

¶ If cry, then cry out.

¶ Out of an excess of concordance, there is this which exposes the workings of a terrible misunderstanding between the body (which one) and its history. The equivalency proposed in the preface to the French translation of *Empirismo eretico*[16] between itself and the simultaneous murder of its author on a beach of Ostia is a false concordance. It betrays its exact betrayal, in the name of a desire for association.

¶ In a text published for the first time in 1969 in *Cinema nuovo* and later included in *Empirismo Eretico*, Pier Paolo Pasolini affirms that "The distance which separates a clap of thunder from a flash of lightning seems incredible [...]. I saw a dubbed version," he continues, "of the stupendous *Tales of the Pale Moon of August* [*Ugetsu Monogatari*], and the words dubbed from Japanese had nothing to do with the persons who were speaking: they produced themselves in two completely different time frames."[17]

¶ A backdraft of time is released on the outcomes of failing organs, a shadow calling its own shadow, its share of mirror, and face. The dull hour of a halophile name unleashed on the humid leagues that hesitate between the surges of charged concrete and the reduced areas secreting gravities.

16. Preface to the French translation of this work by Maria-Antonietta Macciocchi. In English as *Heretical Empiricism*, tr. Ben Lawton and Louise K. Barnett. Bloomington (IN), Indiana University Press. 1988.
17. Translation modified. Pier Paolo Pasolini. « Il cinema e la lingua orale, » in *Cinema Nuovo*, n° 201, sept.-oct. 1969. "Cinema and Oral Language" in English (in *Heretical Empiricism, op. cit.*, p. 264.)

¶ Pasolini's excised sentence insists: "But one must not be taken in by these extreme examples nor by the more normal instances, that is, the majority of cases (films, particularly in Italy, precisely because of the dubbing, are always badly spoken: and the thunder is a sort of regurgitation or yawn which hobbles behind the lightning.)"[18]

¶ And yet the injunction *not to be taken in* is that which *in-tends* for me. The frame is an *emptiness* without being a *void*.[19] If I run, if I dance, it's the same temporality—seized in the image of its disappearance.

¶ The pre-text of Mizoguchi Kenji's film, which conjoins two tales by Ueda Akinari, sustains the echo of an anterior breach in a thatched roof whose aperture is under dispute—in order either, by a night of rain and moon, to procure the pleasure of the patter of the downpour on the hermetic roof, or to leave the piercing exposed in order to admire the aster enveloped in fog.

18. Pier Paolo Pasolini, *Ibid.*
19. In his Nobel prize speech, "Japan, the Beautiful and Myself" (*Utsukushii nihon no watakushi*, 1968), Kawabata Yasunari insists on the distinction between the Japanese *emptiness* and the Occidental *void*: "Here we have the emptiness, the nothingness, of the Orient. My own works have been described as works of emptiness, but it is not to be taken for the nihilism of the West." (Tr. Edward G. Seidensticker, Kodansha Gendai Shinson, 1969). Elsewhere Nishiyama Yuji confirms that "Kawabata admire le vide oriental pratiqué par le moi vague, et n'y voit pas une simple façon nihiliste d'échapper au monde, mais bien l'affirmation singulière du monde." (« Entre le vague et l'ambigu: sur la question du clair/obscur au Japon, » in *Rue Descartes*, 2009/3 (n° 65). (*Kawabata admires the oriental emptiness practised by the vague self, and does not see in it a simple nihilistic way of escaping the world, but very much the singular affirmation of the world.*) According to Jean-Noël Robert, a preferable translation of the title of Kawabata's speech might follow François Berthier's proposal: "The Japanese aesthetic translation out of which I emerged." *Cf.* Jean-Noël Robert. *La hiéroglossie japonaise*. Paris, Collège de France/Fayard, 2012, p. 30.

¶ The real thus exceeded by the facts of Komparu Zenchiku's Nō assumes the form of a roof perforated by the interlacings of two irreconcilable desires, which nonetheless sustain rather than annul one another, and whose landswell transmutes the village house into a pontoon floating on a world that can only assume the figure of a survivor—of itself—incapable of arriving at itself.

¶ The other sentence of the Austrian philosopher cuts in: »Das Subjekt gehört nicht zur Welt, sondern es ist eine Grenze der Welt.«[20] A limit-world that rejects that, precisely, which grants it its defeated form.

¶ It warrants the recusal of complete immersion, or absolute departure, pinning itself at a mutable outlayer that contends a death that is unheard of, that cannot be witnessed, and that is outside of the realms into which it enters and in which it is imprinted.

¶ The *doppia ora* of a vital disagreement suspended in the snare of a perennial expectation.

The body, which one

¶ If it is a word, it is a duplicitous word, because compound, and whose repercussion signals the defeat of seeing such as it is articulated. Because the *historical actualization* (of the

---

20. "The subject does not belong to the world, but it is a limit of the world." Ludwig Wittgenstein, *op. cit.*, p. 94.

body, which one) such as it is formulated by Walter Benjamin rests on a semantic splintering whose consequence, multiply redistributed in French, serves as evidence as to the incommensurability of the present.

¶ The impossibility of receiving the present.

¶ It concerns the *Jetztzeit* of the "Concept of History" declined, in French, by several simultaneous translations—which include:
"now,"
"henceforth,"
"time of the hour,"
"now time"
"actuality,"[21]
—and whose shattering sub-tends and undertakes the exact hour of its abrogation.

¶ Only now, a leaf is lifted by the untimely wave and deposited creased at the foot of the dry wall. This is its indignation: "Reality is given as reality."[22]

---

21. Martin Rueff provides a semantic enumeration of the French translation of the word *Jetztzeit* in « La sœur du rêve, » the prefatory text to his translation of *Odio gli indifferenti* (I hate the indifferent) by Antonio Gramsci, published in 2012 by Payot et Rivages under the title *Pourquoi je hais l'indifférence.*
22. Translation by Michael F. Marra. The line is taken from the poem Kiiroi kao ("Yellow face"), which stages a critique of racism through a dialogue between a European, a positivist Asian thinker and an Asian metaphysician. Michael F. Marra, "A Dialogue on Language between a Japanese and an Inquirer: Kuki Shūzō's Version," in Victor Sōgen Hori and Melissa Anne-Marie Curley (dir.), *Neglected Themes and Hidden Variations, Frontiers of Japanese Philosophy 2* (Nagoya: Nanzan Institute for Religion and Culture, 2008), pp. 56-77.

¶ A testamentary present.

¶ This same word, *reality*, which offers itself as a homologue to the Japanese *genjitsu*, which it translates, is *also* translatable as *actuality*.[23] Thus, the *actual* to which we are ostensibly convoked, here, now, is intractably bound to what is said to be material or concrete, the rough incisure that speaks bruising and tears, a time belonging already to itself, its due.[24] All of which is subject to interpretation, knowing nonetheless that one of the components of the *real* is the *true*, without exigency for verisimilitude.[25]

23.   "In Japan during the 1930s this conflict over realism and abstraction was played out in philosophic speculation and literary criticism over the meaning of terms like *"genjitsu"*—reality—and actuality and what constituted the concrete." Harry Harootunion, "'*Detour to the East': Noël Burch and the Task of Japanese Film*," in *To the Distant Observer: Form and Meaning in the Japanese Cinema*. Also: *The Kanji Dictionary*, dir. Mark Spahn, Wolfgang Hadamitzky, Kimiko Fujie-Winter, p. 823. Tokyo, Tuttle Publishing, 2002 (1996).

24.   Need it be specified that *due* in Italian, is *two*.

25.   Although his senior, Kuki Shūzō was a student of Heidegger's, who later abused Kuki in a contestable text which assumes the English title, "Dialogue on Language with a Japanese and an Enquirer" (tr. P.D. Hertz in *On the Way to Language*). Kuki is also the author, unrecognised by Albert Camus, of an important reflection exploited by The Myth of Sisyphus, attributing to Sisyphus the happiness for which he is known. Cf. « La notion du temps et la reprise sur le temps en orient », a talk given at Pontigny during the summer of 1928, and this unequivocal sentence: « Sisyphe devrait être heureux, étant capable de la répétition perpétuelle de l'insatisfaction. » (Cf. *Annales bergsoniennes VI, Bergson, le Japon, la catastrophe*. PUF. Paris, 2013, p. 54. *Sisyphus should be happy, being capable of the perpetual repetition of dissatisfaction*.) A thinker of Iki, Kuki's relationship to the ultra-nationalism of the Meiji period is subject to controversy. See, on the subject, Graham Parkes, "The Putative Fascism of the Kyoto School and the Political Correctness of the Modern Academy" in Philosophy East and West, July 1997, 47/3, Honolulu, University of Hawai'i Press, 1997. "One must again protest this practice of condemning a Japanese thinker, even at second hand, on the basis of his association with Heidegger. When evaluating philosophical ideas or the integrity of philosophers, assigning 'guilt by association' is as questionable a tactic as it is in the real world of law."

¶ The movement of the *real* carried over onto the *true* is the risk of any attempt at simultaneity, or *resemblance*, never mind *assembly*. It is both the insidious desire for simulation practised by eugenicists of all times (including *today* whether through cloning or assisted reproductive technologies), and the nationalist impulse by which *history* validates itself *uniquely* through antecedence. It is what would call itself *tragic* if it weren't for the faith that motivates it, knowing that tragedy is as much what *breaks* as what is *broken*.

¶ In his notes to screenwriter Yoda Yoshikata, Mizoguchi specifies: "The word: 'I'm going to kill' must be replaced by a threatening gesture." Later he adds: "It is the brutality, the violence of war, that has to be accentuated."[26]

¶ In order to measure the wingspan of a bird, it is laid out on its back, its wings are deployed, and the figure is registered. Ornithologists prefer for the bird to be dead, because of the great risk, otherwise, of breaking a wing.

¶ If the thunderclap is subject to the delays incited by atmospheric doubling, the dubbing of languages and inclemencies, the cry of the chrysanthemum is no less voluble.

¶ The beginnings of Mizoguchi's project, the desire for which, confided to Yoda, is to stage two tales from *Ugetsu monogatari*[27], rest on a misremembrance on the part of the

26. Yoda Yoshikata. *Souvenirs de Kenji Mizoguchi*, tr. Kōichi Yamada, Bernard Béraud and André Moulin. Paris, Cahiers du Cinéma, 1997, p. 105.

27. Ueda Akinari. *Tales of Moonlight and Rain*, tr. Anthony H. Chambers. New York, Columbia University Press, 2007. *"In the late spring of Meiwa 5, on a night*

director, which, once identified, reverberates nonetheless as an aside in the wings of the retained texts—in other words "A Serpent's Lust" and "The Reed-Choked House."[28] If Mizoguchi mistakes "The Reed-Choked House" for another text from the same collection, "The Chrysanthemum Vow," it is in effect only an apparent contradiction, as one story may be read in ghostly relation to the other.[29] While the first relates the peregrinations of a potter who seeks his fortune in a time of war only to return to his village years later where his wife awaits him—in the form of a ghost; the second follows the itinerary of a warrior who commits suicide in order to keep his meeting with the lover to whom he finally presents himself—trans-substantiated.

¶ If the body has the right only to an emaciated form, it is its slide outside of calculated time that gives way to new geographies whose doubling augurs both annulment and escape.

¶ Genjuro's double-entry into the (un-)inhabited house, signals the satisfaction of a departure. An unrealisable arrival. Neither version of the house—*one house and two people*, writes Mizoguchi[30]—is able to propose a complete accounting,

with a misty moon after the rains have cleared, I compose this at my window and give it to the bookseller. The title is 'Tales of Moonlight and Rain.'"(Author's preface under the pseudonym Senshi Kijin.) Chambers specifies in his introduction that *Ugetsu* literally means "rain-moon." (p. 13).

28.   Here I am omitting mention of a third text, by Guy de Maupassant: « La décoration », in the margins of Ueda Akinari's tales. Cf. Yoda Yoshikata, *op. cit.*, p. 103.

29.   « Voici alors la montagne qui se fond; voilà le fleuve qui luit; voici la lune qui rêve; voilà le nuage qui cache tout. » (*Here then is the mountain that dissolves; here is the river that gleams; here is the moon that dreams; here the cloud that hides all.*") Kuki Shūzō, "L'expression de l'infini dans l'art japonais," in *Cahiers de l'Étoile*, janvier-février 1929, Paris, p. 48.

30.   Yoda Yoshikata, *op. cit.*, p. 111.

other than of absence, and this despite its twinned apertures, which prove ultimately to be substractive. Their conjunction depends as much on the split body of the potter. And one wonders to what degree this body (which one) is committed to the murder of Miyagi.[31]

¶ The fact is breach, and breach the very body undone on the same breach by which it is recognised.

¶ Between 1909 and 1910, some sixty years after the development by Louis-Désiré Blanquart-Évrard of albumined paper,[32] a single island of the Hawaian archipelago is the site of a phenomenal killing. In less than a year, the eradication is achieved of more than 300,000 albatrosses whose amputated wings will supply the millinery industry, and whose eggs, withdrawn from the nests of these placid seabirds, will nourish the photography industry at a rate, in the Dresden factory alone, of some 60,000 eggs

31. If *Ugetsu monogatari* is a work of war, a work that revolts against a war that will nonetheless arrive, as a permanent human condition, the circular movements of the figures in the film which appear to return them to a point of departure fall outside of the parameters of either a (joyous) Nietzschean return of the same, or of a symbolically Sisyphean exercise, each of which proposes a fashioning of eternities. The cruel extinctions that traverse *Ugetsu monogatari* owe their impulse to human actions, and are exclusively beholden to themselves. One need only consider the double-doors hanging from the hinges of the abandoned palace of Lady Wakasa's demonic splendor, cast in the carefully elaborated shadows of Nō, the intensification of which is inscribed in the traits of a face become a darkened mask; the doors leading in and out of worlds. If the phantoms—whether, of Miyagi, Lady Wakasa, or the near-phantom of the boatman— exert themselves within the living architectures of perception, disrupting any certainty as to the exactitude of the frontier between the vital palpitant body and the bodies in the bone-yard, it is that they have made ghosts of the living.
32. Louis-Désiré Blanquart-Évrard. *Traité de photographie sur papier*. Paris, Librairie encyclopédique de Roret, 1851.

per day.[33] The pelagic desolation, echoed over the waves, receives as a sole response to its complaint the photographic documentation of its quasi-total extermination.[34]

¶ If elsewhere, at another moment of writing, following the ransacked roof and the dispersed gulls, the dismembered trees with their great trunks laid upon the dilapidated beach, and before even the idea of a war (since without discontinuity), an idea that levies and leverages itself, an author was able to declare with conviction: "My life [...] is a crime story without slaughter, without cops or victims, without a single subject,"[35] it is that the pains given to montage, its summation, is a species without recourse to identification, and for which *everything* depends upon its disappearance.

¶ The just measure of a bird cannot be calculated, if not in flight.

33. Beaumont Newhall. "60,000 Eggs a Day" in *Image*, vol. 4, no 4 (April 1955). This number does not only represent albatross eggs. It is to be noted, as well, that, cited by way of example, this killing represents a very small percentage of birds assassinated to various ends at the turn of the twentieth century, entailing the near total obliteration of the populations of shorebirds and seabirds whose feathers are destined to the same markets. According to a report prepared in 1911 by researchers from the University of Iowa having travelled to Laysan Island where the task befell them to document the avian presence there—which did not prevent them either from "collecting" several samples—the island carried the traces of the spoliation of poachers one of whose "methods" consisted in tearing off the wings of still living birds leaving them to bleed to death.

34. Paul Virilio having attended to the martial dimension of the cinema, and others like Edward Burtinsky, having attempted an exposé of the ecological damage tied to photography, it remains nonetheless that the devastation inflicted on avian, as well as animal, populations continues largely to be passed over in silence.

35. Marguerite Duras. *La vie matérielle*, Paris, Gallimard [P.O.L.], 1987, p. 157.

ARTEFACTS

: nos me duele el fondo de los ojos,

JULIO CORTÁZAR

It's All True

The *jangadeiros* are sailors who inhabit the *Nordeste* of Brazil. In the 1940's, having built a sailing raft of bound logs, a representative group of four jangadeiros navigated the 2,000 perilous kilometres of the Brazilian coast separating them from Rio de Janeiro where they requested an audience with the president (dictator) of the time, Getúlio Doneles Vargas, with the intention of improving their crushing working conditions. The audience was granted as were the jangadeiros's requests. Orson Welles, whose itinerary, by incitement of the Brazilian government (department of Tourism), and in collaboration with the U.S. Office of Inter-American Affairs, led him to Brazil in 1942 to make a propagandistic film, became interested in the story of the jangadeiros. Turning away from his dubious diplomatic mission, Welles set about making a segment of his painfully uncompleted film *It's All True*. The four jangadeiros who undertook the historic voyage were to represent themselves in their own roles. During filming, an accident claimed the life of jangadeiro Manoel Olimpio Meira, alias Jacaré, whose brother ended up doubling him in order to complete the sequence, the exaltation of which was tempered by Jacaré's *actual* death.

Four Men on a Raft says with stupefaction the
impossibility of restatement, against every
promise made by reproducible technology.
By allowing a glimpse of the torn lining of
history, it is an elegy of an elegy, the origin
of which it will have been the incitement.

Watabe Yukichi
In 1958, the photographer Watabe Yukichi
was granted the permission to document
the inquest led by the Tokyo Police into the
"affair of the cut up body." The narrative
that follows is extracted from the book *A
Criminal Investigation*:
"In July 1958, a special nationwide police
campaign was launched, the first of its kind,
during which data of 21 unsolved murder
cases were compared by all law-enforce-
ment agencies. This investigation led to
the identification of a hitherto unidentified
corpse, which had been found in Kurashiki
(Okayama Prefecture) in February 1956. The
body was that of Miura Shofu. Curiously
enough, Miura was still registered as being
alive and it was at this point that the police
understood that they were dealing with a

case of [stolen identity].[36, 37] Miura turned
out to be Onishi Katsumi, who was arrested
on July 16th, 1958 and confessed his crimes.
He had in fact committed four murders: on
June 1st, 1955, he had poisoned his adop-
tive parents Onishi Fukumatsu and his
wife Kuma at their home in Shimonoseki
(Yamaguchi Prefecture) using cyanide. He
then fled to Hokkaido where he worked on a
food-stall under a false name before making
his way to Tokyo. Here he befriended Miura
Shofu, persuaded him to sell him his iden-
tity card for 40,000 Yen and murdered him
in order to adopt Miura's identity. He mar-
ried, and got a job in a cardboard-box factory.
The subsequent murder of Sato Tadashi was
an attempt to adopt yet another identity."[38]
Of Miura's body, a nose was found, two pha-
langes, as well as a member: his sex. Several
cut fingers are missing. Of the face, there is

36. Bœder's translation prefers the expression "identi-
ty-theft," language that only entered English usage in the
limited context of espionage in 1964 but didn't gain wider
usage until the 1990's, hence my preference here for the less
contemporary expression "stolen identity," which preserves
something also of a cinematic reference.
37. "He was living under a borrowed name. [...] And this
makes for a man even more alone than other men." Marguerite
Duras, La douleur. P.O.L. Éditeur. Paris, 1985.
38. "Onishi Katsumi was found guilty of his crimes on
December 23rd, 1959. On March 30th, 1961 the death
sentence was confirmed and Onishi was executed in 1965."
Titus Bœder, in Watabe Yukishi, A Criminal Investigation.
Xavier Barral et Le BAL. Paris, 2011.

left only the cloud of acid used to destroy its
traits. The body thus defaced was found "on
the other side of the lake."[39]

Neither Miura's face nor his body were
photographed by Watabe; if such a photo
does exist, it was not published in the series
of the investigation of the cut up body.
One of the photographs, cropped, severs
the arm of a police officer, behind whom a
windowed door is visible.

The Devonian
After fifty-seven million years, the Devonian
was declared missing. This occurred some
three-hundred-and-sixty million years ago,
following the advent of leaves, and roots,
and sandy lagoons. Flowers had not yet
appeared. This period corresponds to the
important *emergence from the water*. Adam
Sedgwick, one of the founders of modern
geology, and teacher of Charles Darwin,
proposed an interpretation of geological
formations, notably, of south-western
England. Addressing the Devonian ques-
tion, Sedgwick's biographers, John Willis

39. It is impossible, by the current vagaries of my reading,
not to relate this crime to Kawabata's novel, *Mizuumi* (The
Lake), 1955 (1974 for the English translation) and to Gimpei's
fantasies.

Clark and Thomas McKenny Hughes affirm, in 1890, that: "The rocks of the northern part of the Devon promontory lie in a trough-like fold running east and west, so that the older rocks turn up along the Bristol Channel, and again on the south along a line running roughly west from Exeter to the sea. [...] Neither of these two series was found to be exactly like the rocks which occurred on the other side of the channel about the horizon where these might be expected." Preoccupied by the difference between two groups of mineral matter, they add: "It therefore became necessary to consider whether any of these Devon beds were the geological equivalents of deposits thrown down under different conditions in the adjoining area of Wales, and, when there was a likeness, whether some of them might after all have only an accidental resemblance to the strata with which they had been hitherto identified."[40]

Be that as it may, the body, constitutionally capsized, is submitted to the reiterative cinema of its extraction.

40. *The Life and Letters of Adam Sedgwick, Volume I*, dir. John Willis Clark et Thomas McKenny Hughes. Cambridge, Cambridge University Press, 2009 (1890), pp. 537-538.

The arm

The background actor twice tenders her arm to have her blood taken. The first time the blood spurts. The second time, it runs. Twice, then, lies as to sequence and simultaneity. What is given to see, is neither the arm, nor the bloodletting, but a consequence of time. The only take is the one shown.

It comes down to the face.

A face that is both substantial and substitutive. The face, for example, of Jeanne d'Arc in Dreyer's film. His only great passion. There exist two negatives of the film: the Oslo negative and the contested Lo Duca negative which for many years supplanted the first, especially overseas. If doubling is an effect, not to say a practice, of the cinema, it is no less true that it enjoys a use that is far more widespread than is often recognized. In the 1920's it was common practice, for cinematographers, in order not to wear out the negative of the film (which would become increasingly degraded with each development), to place two cameras side by side that filmed, simultaneously, the sequences of a film, with, of course, a slight delay, both machines being incapable of occupying the same space at the same time. This delay is visible in Dreyer, when the Oslo negative is placed next to the Lo Duca negative. If one or the other

contest the idea of an originary film, not-
withstanding the director's selections, it is
no less true that the spectator is persistently
afflicted with a kind of *double vision*. A trou-
bled vision whose composite characteristics,
which overlay the faces delivered in close-up
to make them into a single indefinite (and
not eternal) face transmuted into pain, car-
ries the mark of the irreceivable. Because the
doubling which blurs Jeanne d'Arc's face with
the monk Massieu's is assignation to the fall
in question. A profoundly atheist fall, and
which is owed to a recanted, inaudible, lure.

If the flutter reaches the image in decline,
the body that befalls it is subject to that very
same body's protests. Its ramifications touch
the ground, and are only visible in winter,
in the light of a glacial sun. As for the sea,
it isolates the detail of an intractable ache. It
speaks a skin, into its tear.

Blow-Up

What body bespeaks the *prima facie*? What
death bespeaks the first impression?
If, as Nietzsche suggests, "'appearance' is a
word that contains many temptations," it is
to be avoided "as much as possible." "For,"
he insists, "it is not true that the essence of

things 'appears' in the empirical world."[41]
Is it then necessary to limit, if not de-lim-
it, oneself, by setting aside the truth that
speaks false, to "appearance and unreality"[42]
following, for example, a certain Michel,
translator and photographer, as it happens
the late narrator of "Las babas del diablo,"[43] a
short work by Julio Cortázar. If Antonioni's
film reinstalls the secondary effects of the
narrative in a fixed, locatable, criminalis-
able, context, Cortázar's short story refuses
the distinction precisely between crime and
its sexed disposition: the conjugated marks
of translation and photography whose
imprecision is of all hours, and whose
morbidity is continually attested by its pal-
pitating *überleben*, its *sur-vival* (over-life).
The instigation of the slippage, incessantly
formulated—and belied—by one and other
of these vocations is beholden to the fact that
"every looking oozes with mendacity, because
it's that which expels us further *outside our-*

41. Friedrich Nietzsche. *Philosophy and Truth: Selections
from Nietzsche's Notebooks of the early 1870's*, tr. Daniel
Breazeale. New Jersey, Humanities Press International,
1979, p. 86. Both Angèle Kremer-Marietti and Nils Gascuel,
independently of one another, translate *phénomène* where
Breazeale translates *appearance*.
42. Here, Breazeale's translation reads "illusion and
unreality."
43. Las babas del diablo signifies *the devil's drool* and refers
idiomatically to spider threads, or to the filaments of dew that
interlace strands of grass or plants.

selves.[44] The falsehood on which the lying truth depends, extended along exhausted distances. Fine rain upon a lens.

Death, un-executed

In 1985, when the remains of Joseph Mengele, who had eluded Mossad's agents at the time of Adolf Eichmann's arrest in Buenos Aires, are exhumed, in a municipality of São Paolo, the identification of his skeleton demands recourse to new forensic procedures that draw notably on photographic, sometimes cinematographic processes.[45] It was a matter of reading the narrative of the remains against its fiction in order to draw a mute testimony from the ventriloquized thing, whose voice, thrown to the sea, returned to its genocidal charge. To translate the probability of its identity into justice. According to Thomas Keenan and Eyal Weizman, "[...] the bones of a skeleton are exposed to life in a similar way that photographic film is exposed to light. A life, understood as an extended set of exposures to a myriad of forces (labor, location, nutrition, violence, and so on), is projected

44. Julio Cortázar. *Blow-Up and Other Stories*, tr. Paul Blackburn. New York, Pantheon Books, 1967 [1963], p. 119. My emphasis.
45. These same procedures will serve in the sbsequent identification of the *desaparecidos* of Latin-American, African and Balkan dictatorships.

onto a mutating, growing and contracting negative, which is the body in life."[46] More specifically the face,[47] for it is the face of the presumed Joseph Mengele, or his skull, that was to dislocate the enigma, with the help of a machine developed by the West-German scientist Richard Helmer, which enabled a series of images to be projected onto the *actual*, in other words tempo-material, skull of the SS-Hauptsturmführer, at different angles, in order to reveal the concordance between bone structure and the flesh that vested it, *beyond a reasonable doubt.* In other words, an elaborate procedure of doubling was undertaken in order to arrive at the criminal body having, thanks to the Austrian couple Wolfram and Liselotte Bossert, been exempted from history.

Mengele, just like Le Corbusier two years hence, died swimming in the open waters. This took place at Embu das Artes, in Brasil. If one grants Embu a slide toward French, it bespeaks the very saturation that is here in question. Recourse to the second definition of *embu* offered by the *Littré* (1880) dictionary,

46. *Mengele's Skull.* Berlin / Frankfurt-Am-Main, Sternberg Press / Portikus, 2012, p. 20.

47. "The face made up for the very first time," (Kawabata Yasunari, tr. composite from Sylvie Regnault-Gatier et al. and Edward Seidensticker. In English, *House of the Sleeping Beauties*, tr. E. Seidensticker. Tokyo / Palo Alto, Kodansha Intl, 1969, p. 148).

reveals: "Saturation of the soil of cemeteries, condition that arises from the fact that, new corpses having been incessantly inhumed before the older corpses have had time to consume themselves, the ground becomes ill-suited to operate the changes that constitute putrefaction."

Against a Green Sky

In 1960, Oshima Nagisa determined to make a film without inclusion of the colour green. Without allowing glimpses either of the sky over the roofs of houses, for these images give the pernicious feeling of a small satisfaction that "this is good enough." If "the blue sky above the brown earth is sufficient to teach us the terror of human life,"[48] he writes, the sky beyond the green of the pine trees is a form of panacea. This recalls Antonioni's unremitting decision to have a whole forest painted in order to accede to a certain effect of light—a vain effort, since the sky cleared before the shoot, destroying the very possibility of the effect destined to an abandoned passage of *Il Deserto Rosso*. Oshima declares in this same text on the banishment of green that he has "a definite

48. Oshima Nagisa. "Banishing Green" in *Cinema, Censorship and the State, 1956-1978,* tr. Dawn Lawson. Cambridge (MA), MIT Press, 1991, p. 210.

distrust of the architects and others who
create Japan's scenery, particularly because
they have not created even one place with
scenery that adequately negates reality."[49]
R., the condemned Korean in *Koshikei* (in
English as *Death by Hanging*), a 1968 film
based on a news chronicle that mobilised
the Japanese intelligentsia against the death
penalty, asks, as he regains consciousness,
after his assassination by the state and before
its reprisal: "What is a nation?" "I don't want
to be murdered," he declares, "for an abstrac-
tion."[50] The double murder committed in the
name of the state is reiterated in a reality that
is precisely exacerbated by the imaginary.
A vicious imaginary, and through which
the formal agents of the prison put them-
selves in the place of the condemned man
in an absurd theatrical attempt to revive his
memory—or rather to saturate themselves
with his memory such as it is transcribed
in the court proceedings—, to the point of
tearing down the wall of propriety between
desire and its actualisation; with their hands
inside their pants, they salivate on the bodies
of the young murdered women and gloat with
murderous envy intricated in reminiscences
of war (gratuitous killings) and in simulated

49. *Ibid.*, p. 211.
50. Oshima Nagisa. *Koshikei* (Death by Hanging), bxw,
1968 (117:00).

rapes committed against one another, with a bottle between their legs in the guise of a godemiche. In contra-band, when they leave, unvested, the small typical house in which the hangings take place according to a strict ritual which is abused by the petty functionary assassins, one hears the intonations, over their heads, and over the clothes floating on the lines, through the crackling crowd, the Sieg Heil of the Deutsches Reich.

CROSSFALL

—*I think I see a ship out there.*
—*Yes*
—*A ship whose mast is split in two.*

Akutagawa Ryūnosuke

~

It is by the necropolis that life is made discernible. By the absence of water that the rivers of old are prognosticated. And by the flooding of the Tiber that the ancient forum is identified.

Janiculum.

The anterior name of the city of Roma Antica which preceded Roma città, city of first bridges. A city "in which the river, overtaking the last hills, approaches the coastal and alluvial fringe efflorescing through the low lands,

What I have to tell you must be kept from its secret.

I was to begin with a single body, stretched out along the hemispheres. Unexpected, as it is said of window ledges or the disappearance of the tides, of winged creatures that enter into you, introducing thin trickles of bloodshed; strange signalling for the ocean liners of the drowned citadels, little white flag with its stain, it had been a century, an undressed centurion who hammered the top floor with his stallions, and this is how the voyage came undone, on the incisure of a highly plagiarised sea.

ill-suited to the establishment of a road edging the sea, and at which point it is no longer passable. This first bridge neighbouring the port as far as which the boats can rise along the river and where the maritime traffic makes contact with terrestrial traffic."[51]

Between two sea walls, a swamp stagnates, which, despite efforts to drain it, the Tiber rejects onto its shores. Roma Antica, city of plains, is a latent marsh.

51. Amable Audin. "Naissance de Rome" in *Revue de Géographie de Lyon*, Volume XXXI, No 1, 1956, p. 21. Here, Audin is citing the research findings of Joël Le Gall.

The depth of its buried name Janiculum, from Janus, god of openings, of beginnings and time, leads a subterranean path to the crowd gathered before the door toward which the torrent of the stairwell pours, and the manifest body, torn from the fields and the wells, from the rivers and the volcanic mouths, all the way to the letter in a state of arrest.

A drowning in the lands. This too is possible.

(I close the shutters and leave the world
alone with the silver of its skies.)

PIER PAOLO PASOLINI

Pasolini's Our recasts texts spoken at Institut du Tout-Monde (Université Paris I Panthéon Sorbonne, June 2014), and at Université de Montréal (May 2015, April 2016) and the fragmentary reprisal of which produced a seminar delivered in June 2016 at the School of the Art Institute of Chicago; several passages published in les *Cahiers Artaud N° 2* appear here as well. With due recognition to Sylvie Glissant, Cathy Delpech, Alain Jugnon, Andrea Oberhuber, Barbara Agnese and Gregg Bordowitz for these openings which formed veritable encounters. I wish also to name my friendship with Hervé Sanson to whom some of the pages of this *Our* are addressed.

It is with much emotion that I dedicate these drowned leaves to Stephen Motika
&
to Myriam Suchet.
(July 2016)

Epigraphs

With the exception of Wittgenstein (tr. C.K. Ogden, Frank Ramsay + Wittgenstein) and Akutagawa (tr. Charles de Wolf), epigraphs are all translated by the author from existing French translations, i.e. Pasolini (tr. Hélène Frappat); Bachmann (tr. Miguel Couffon), Kuki Shūzō (tr. Omodaka Hisyuki). The closing epigraph by Pasolini is translated by Nathanaël in correspondence with Jennifer Scappettone.

Translations

Unattributed translations are the author's.

Photograph

Clarence Albrecht, Albatross wings piled in old guano shed, Laysan Island, 1911. *Biological Survey—Bulletin No. 42*, U.S. Department of Agriculture, May 21, 1912.

ELEMENTS OF A PHOTOGRAPH OF TRANSLATION

Pasolini's Our owes its existence to an echo trapped inside an amphitheatre in the 15ᵗʰ arrondissement of Paris. In other words, it owes its life to a death which preceded it, and which will never be finished anticipating it.

It was approached under another title—*Elements of a photograph of translation*—and it was at S.'s suggestion that its first subdued word was spoken at the Institut du Tout-Monde, at Paris I (Panthéon-Sorbonne), where C. couldn't make it because of a rail strike that prevented her from leaving Perpignan. It is nonetheless the case that this text took its first steps in Paris, after having been written in a dark room in Edgewater, poisoned by the nauseant stench rising from the building's courtyard. It was a matter of *saying*, out loud, photography's exposure to translation. The first pieces of evidence gathered to this effect were the French translation of several essays by Pier Paolo Pasolini and the elements comprising the Berlin Wall, but the cinema as well, as such, (by which I mean the cinematographic cinema, with its friable and sometimes inflamed film). It was necessary, before these facts, to identify as well the doubling (dubbing) that *undertook* the montages such as they were named, whether cinematic or otherwise. The albatross had not yet manifested as an individual.

The title was eventually displaced, and stopped for a time at *Pas de pluie dans Pasolini* (this one did not make it into

English) before arriving at the *Our* in hand. All of which, with the help of Mizoguchi Kenji, whom Pasolini names, under the very rain evacuated from his own cinema. The beach is dry, like the marsh it signifies. And the chrysanthemum clutches in its furl a most intimate of enigmas for the body that recognises itself there.

It is pointless for me to advance any explanation whatsoever for this work; it would always be *retrospective*. But I may say without lying, that this book was written *despite myself*. And if I thought that I was writing for this or that talk, a text on Claude Cahun or on Ingeborg Bachmann, I had to recognise, after several terrible months of defeat, that *everything* I had written since 2014, when Europe toppled (it was the World Cup, the métro Barbès was closed for obviously racist reasons, the camera operator did not deprive herself of several remarks in that direction, and Sunday morning, on the way to the Cinémathèque, the métro Gare de l'Est was armed to the teeth—the incidents in The Hague, etc., would soon follow), prolonging this same *criminal investigation*. As for the aeroplane, it took off as planned for New York, the streets were crowded, in the absence of T., and the canal covered in filth, which O. was similarly able to observe. I would be incapable of affirming, since then, what this made of the *book* such as I understand it, nor of writing as such. If it recuses a form of logic, it defends its secret, from which it expulses even its author. The book was made, then, in a way, *in the absence of its author*, who found herself proscribed just like any reader, from the writing she was making of the text which reverted to her and to which would be attached her signature.

There are islands which disappear in the tides. Their reappearance inscribes in the field of one's vision a *new* island which never shall be repeated. It is to such an island that I owe my drowning in January 2010 on the southwest coast of Martinique. If it is impossible, despite forensic attempts at reconstruction, to account for the damage to a place, it is even more vain to go in search of a body. And no burial place, even provisional, will re-establish for it a nominal present. Because it is never the same body, and no translation will preserve it from that outcome.

Nathanaël
Chicago, March 15, 2018

NATHANAËL is the author of more than a score of books written in English or in French, and published in the United States, Québec, and France.

NIGHTBOAT BOOKS

Nightboat Books, a nonprofit organization, seeks to develop audiences for writers whose work resists convention and transcends boundaries. We publish books rich with poignancy, intelligence, and risk. Please visit nightboat.org to learn more about us and how you can support our future publications.

The following individuals have supported the publication of this book. We thank them for their generosity and commitment to the mission of Nightboat Books:

Elizabeth Motika
Benjamin Taylor

In addition, this book has been made possible, in part, by grants from the New York State Council on the Arts Literature Program and the Topanga Fund, which is dedicated to promoting the arts and literature of California.